I Never Saw My Dad'

Skye + Fam

Dedication

In loving memory of our Baba Farasat,
we dedicate this book to all the amazing dads and father figures!

We see you.

Acknowledgments

We are thankful for our Dads, grandfathers, father figures, and male role models in our lives.

I never saw my Dad's cape, but...

I see him move big, heavy cans.
He makes things that are hard for me to do look so easy.

I see him work in the yard on weekends.
He makes maintaining our house look so easy.

I see him play with me in the big, blue ocean.
He makes being fearless look so easy.

I see him wash our car.
He makes cleaning look so easy.

I see him workout often.
He makes exercising look so easy.

I see him take his vitamins every day.
He makes taking care of himself look so easy.

I see him enjoy fresh foods whenever he can.
He makes eating healthy look so easy.

I see him whisper a 'thank you' for his meal.
He makes being grateful look so easy.

I see him meditate every morning before work.
He makes keeping good habits look so easy.

I see him learn to ride a motorcycle.
He makes trying something new look so easy.

I see him on a Zoom call with a lot of people.
He makes being a boss look so easy.

I saw him prepare meals for us after long workdays.
He makes cooking at home look so easy.

I see him call Grandma on Friday evenings.
He makes keeping family traditions look so easy.

I see him build a chicken coop with spare materials.
He makes building things look so easy.

I see him woodworking.
He makes being creative look so easy.

I see him sad at times.
He makes going through tough times look so easy.

∴

I see him give me his pasta, so I'd be full.
He makes knowing when to put my needs first look so easy.

I see him play his guitar at a wedding.
He makes being confident look so easy.

I see him struggle to do magic tricks,
but he does the magic show with me anyway.
He makes sticking through it look so easy.

I see him work hard on his big presentation.
He makes preparing look so easy.

I see him study on weekends and nights.
He makes growing look so easy.

I see him make birthdays and milestones feel so special.
He makes celebrating others look so easy.

I never saw your cape, but ...
Daddy, I see you make everything look so easy.

If you could only see yourself through my eyes,
through the eyes of a little one in this big world
that is made for big people!

None of those things that you do are easy for me.
I remember when you told me once that they were not
easy for you either in the beginning.

Some things are still not easy for you to juggle
and do as perfectly as I know you want them to be.

But Daddy, you do them anyway.

I never saw your cape, but ... I see you.
You are there every day making it happen.

I never saw your cape, but...

I see you _____

You make _____ look so easy.

I see you _____

You make _____ look so easy.

I see you _____

You make _____ look so easy.

I see you _____

You make _____ look so easy.

You make everything look so easy. I see you.

Happy Your-day!

Love, _____

Photo area:
Dad and child or just Dad doing something he loves

About the Author

I Never Saw My Dad's Cape, But ... is co-authored by Skye + Fam: Skye, Payel, and Joe Farasat.

Skye Farasat, age nine, co-authored her third book I Never Saw My Dad's Cape, But ... with her family. Skye came up with the initial concept of the book while secretly observing her Dad meditate every morning before work. In this book, she serves as a little guide who reminds us of the many little (and big) things that Dads (and father figures) do for their families. We may think that the little things go unnoticed and the big things are just little; however, Skye reminds us that our children are always observing us and soaking it all in. Skye has been meditating with her parents since she was a baby. She shares her simple yet powerful technique of using observation as one way to remain mindful and thankful for your dad. Skye is a fourth grader and has been a student of Waldorf education since age four. Since Waldorf's pedagogy centers around inner work, Skye leaves a special space at the end of the book for kids to be inspired to write about how they see their dads.

Payel and Joe Farasat are Skye's mommy and daddy, and they helped edit the book. They are Financial Services executives, certified in coaching, consulting, and mindfulness.

About the Book

A book about celebrating Dads every day! I Never Saw My Dad's Cape, But ... reminds us of the many little (and big) things that Dads (and father figures) do for their families. We may think that the little things go unnoticed and the big things are just little; however, this book reminds us that our children are always observing us and soaking it all in.

The book leaves a special space at the end for kids to be inspired to write about how they see and appreciate their dad. A heartfelt and thoughtful personal dedication makes for a memorable gift for Dad, especially on Father's Day or birthday!

Made in the USA
Las Vegas, NV
26 July 2024

92989787R00036